Also by Seanín Hughes

Little Deaths (Smithereens Press, 2019)

SHE, SHAPESHIFTER

Hughes

ISBN: 978-1-915079-11-4

Cover designed by Aaron Kent

Edited and typeset by Aaron Kent

Broken Sleep Books Ltd
Rhydwen,
Talgarreg,
SA44 4HB
Wales

Contents

She, Shapeshifter

Seanín Hughes

Xenolith

Let me give you something. It begins
with scalpel, pickaxe. I promise
this will not be a pretty sight.
I'll let you in beneath the ribs, make
a clean cut. Bring the axe—
burrow deep, until you reach
the bedrock.

This is where we left off. This
necrotic rock stump,
bound in blue marble; this
is yours.

Russian Dolls

Before breasts,
your poetry is peaches

& cream in cornflower dress,
a doll-cask of sweet sap.

Then, the thrum of blood;
you are on the cusp,

your pupils black moons
bringing the tide.

You are a red creature
bound at the wrists by biology,

your poetry is puce and vermilion—
a ripening lacuna lush

for the splitting of cells,
the giving of yourself

to a body
within a body.

Posthumous Narrative

Here's what I know: he was a war hero,
decorated for serving time at sea.
His hair was slicked into tight curls
the colour of curdled milk. Sour.
Neck tucked into stiff collars, smart navy tie,
Sunday best dressed at all times.

Or, that he was fond
of flashing silk stockings at children,
one of them my mother.

Or, that the rooms in that house
are screaming caskets, home to the ghosts
of girls who knew too much.

Or, that there are infinite possible worlds,
and in them all, he is the same.

Punch, Pray, Rinse, Repeat

Every Tuesday, this woman comes and lights a candle
under Our Lady of Perpetual Help.
I saw her once
on the bus beside a pot-bellied pale girl
wearing a black eye.

Jane at the bingo says *there's no Da—*
slips her tongue around the scandal like
it's apple tart. Smacks her lips.
The Ma bate the child out of her
with her bare fists.

There she is now. See? Praying.
The flame licks her fingers clean.

A History of Love Letters

Miss said every time I told a lie,
Baby Jesus had a nail hammered
                into his hand.

She said I had a *sad mouth*,
corners downturned, pointing
                to hell.

Stephen had a mouth like sunshine.
I gave him a token,
                a tiny toy dinosaur egg,
                pale blue and gold.
I wrote his name on my hand and hoped
the egg would hatch.

My body grew and Granny said, *never
shave your legs*—so I did. Better bald
                spring chicken; better descaled,
plucked bare for boys with nervous fingers
to work me open.

The one who wrote love letters spilled
his entrails in black biro, telling me
                in no particular order
the parts he liked best—some illustrated.

When Napoleon begged his Josephine to lay
                herself bare, he meant for her flaws
to fold her into neat and precious squares;
                for her to be less
than his clenched fist heart could hold.

In place of a filigree pen, my hands
hold pistachios peeping from the lips
of yawning oatmeal shells,
                    ripe and given up easily
for a hungry mouth that isn't my own.

Gathering in the Head
(or, the Perils of Novel Reading)

To begin, she gathered purity. This required
an intimate learning of invisible ropes,
coarse braids coded in knots like braille.
She gathered the gift of a name,
rooted in father: daughter of, property of,
planted in a glass box with dolls, daisies,
pirouettes, pink dresses, etiquette. Pretty thing.
Mild thing. *Sweet thing, does she sing?*

Grew gold thistle between her thighs,
greenbrier in her belly.
Realised pain as prescription. Gathered language,
wrote herself at night in the mist
of her breath by candlelight—erased it.
Gathered fear.

Gathered broad hips, small shoulders, breasts,
full lips to paint and paint worship with. Grew modesty
and virtue, grew into a curved and luscious rib.
Gathered value, voyeurs; appraisals. Got a promise
from a learned, bearded man.

Gathered the same gift twice, renamed, loose roots
in a new lineage: wife of, property of,
validated by. Gathered her ropes
and took them with her. He voyaged insatiably
and found her gold; fancied himself Midas—
multiplied it ten-fold. She gathered porcelain cherub mouths
to pour herself into, not one drop wasted.
Gathered age, stale water: scooped it out from under
her tongue and asked its name. Grew thirsty.

Gathered fjords in her pupils, nostril ravines, every vein
a river, each ear a sea-save for cuttlefish to bleed
their ink. Chartered ships captained
by scandalous women to cross her channels,
carve out canals, skinny dip in her lakes.
Gathered multitudes. Gulped rain deep into the well
of her skull, each drop dripping rotund vowels,
toothy consonants, chiffonade ellipses.
She could not stop. Looked outside: the moon
a puppeteer of tides,
tipping her poles.

Echoes

It begins, ends and begins. Memory births memory in shades
of purple: berry-picking out back in the inevitable autumn
with its bruised fruit and knees, waiting for alchemy
to boil and sweeten in the pot.

The thought fades, slow as a bloodstain you'll never bleach,
and another begins: the ceremonial steeping of teacups,
the whirr of the washing machine, the cleansing and stripping
away of the day's dust. Peeling Kerr's Pinks, blessed balls
of flour, and now she's almost here again—hair coiled in
rollers, cigarette perched on the ashtray, eating itself.

You wonder at the permanence of ghosts, how their mist
seeps and insists on living, somehow, while everything else
is temporary—even where the memory rests, catches
its breath in a handmade wooden box, beside her amethyst
earrings and silver Celtic cross.

Butchers Use Bandsaws

(after Good Bones, by Maggie Smith)

Remember when you told me how butchers
use bandsaws to grind the bones of carcasses
while upstairs, our baby girl slept
and I thought all at once
of what violent creatures we are;
smashed windpipes, crushed corpses, bagged kittens—
everywhere a multitude of deaths—
and I thought of how easily I could
smash a windpipe, crush a coffin, drown a bag of kittens
if it meant keeping my children
from what violent creatures we are.

Other Mother

Tell me your love is cleaved to your chest by Palomar knot
and knuckles pale as plum blossom; how your child
is a chalice full to the brim, perfect. Tell me you are afraid

of your child ever being *other,* unknown quantity.
Ask me about being *other.* Ask me.
I'll tell you I am afraid of someone else's language;

words that roll around my mouth like a stone.
Diagnosis. Progressive. Mucopolysaccharidosis.
Not-yet-loss. Someday loss. Prognosis. Ask me

and I'll tell you I'm afraid of alien vials
needling into her jugular vein, of every blood droplet
that leaks from beneath her skin. I am *other mother* –

meds dispenser, limb restrainer, silent witness,
sombre womb, someday grieving,
always *other* mother.

She, Shapeshifter

The truth is in the kitchen, hidden
under half-nibbled pizza crusts
and sodden teabags.
Ten grime choked half-moons, torn
from nail beds in the numb hours
between night feeds,
no sleep.

The fingers—now indelicate stumps—
crawl through hair damp
with week-long neglect, rustling
at the root, searching for whatever
was there before. They whisper,
why can't I be gentle
with the person I've become?

Divinations

The candle has come to make a church of my bathroom.

Truth drains from my bladder into a glass and in the mirror,
I am bewitched and beautiful.

I borrow the glow of the flame, tiny living thing
with heart and root, rise and fall,

and dip my fingers in its light before swirling a white, plastic
stick in my urine.

The *tick-tick-tick* echoes in the hollow of my throat
and plays percussive tricks

with my heart's rhythm. It talks to the candle
and makes it dance.

Miniature fire fairy, elemental alchemist, primal prayer
to defy the hungry black;

I know you.
Climb inside my womb and illuminate the flesh.

Light me up and leaven my marrow.
The rain is coming.

I Want You to Know that You Are Alive

The natural law is that sometimes,
this must hurt. You will find yourself
hurled headlong into a mound of salt,
skin raw, inside out. And you will know, then,
what it means to be the wound—
what it means to learn how to breathe
through it all.
Know that it is a bravery to live
at full capacity; fill each lung
with equal measure of dark and light.
Drink every cup dry.
Know that nothing is ordinary,
and all things are temporary—
we can never outrun this bittersweet truth.
But, a secret: we can stop, for a moment, and taste it,
unafraid of the sting. It's easier
when you know it's coming;
when you lean into the fall, go limp,
and let the cushion of your knowing
absorb the impact. You will heal
again and again, until.
You will.

Then Again ...

. . . we could pull the tongues from clamouring bells
& leave their houses hollow,
stretch silence taut like a drum skin, stuff the mouths
of prophets with roses, run wild as lines
in the palms of witches, or we could
reverse to become the barefoot, burning child—
go back, back to birth; climb inside the womb's
closed fist; wish to resume the rich dark
& unlearn our failing human codes.

Covenant

I will love this body
first, before loving another,
before loving anything else.

I owe it this much, now
it shows signs of being
simply tired.

Body, I am sorry.

Body, I promise
to stop the punishment.

Let me give you water.

We'll wear our silver rings again,
and that *Ruby Woo lipstick*.

I am ending the battle:
this is a white flag, waving.

We are growing old.
I'll take you with me.

Pretty Vacant

The eclipse has ended
and you are a fragment, as before
with no place here
anymore.
See this delicious space?

--cooled by absent air, empty
of never-there,
vacant, wide open and gorgeous.
Fuck you all. I'll starfish
in this glass bed ripe for filling.

Acknowledgements

I owe a debt of gratitude to the following publications for their support with many of the poems contained in She, Shapeshifter: Abridged, Banshee, Poethead, Under the Radar, and Iamb.

To my children, Naiomh, Aoife, Layne and Áine for tolerating the relentless absurdity that must be having a poet for a mother. To my parents, Patricia and Seamus, and my siblings, Chris and Katrina, for being who you all are. To my partner Stephen, who is a talented gift of a human being.

Thanks and love also to the English faculty at Ulster University in Coleraine and all the friends I made there; Wendy Pratt, Maria McManus, Chris Murray and Dr Kathleen McCracken; my stablemates at Broken Sleep, especially Alice Kinsella and Stuart McPherson, and everyone else whose paths have crossed with mine over the last few years. If I wrote all the names, it would be another book.

Lastly, thank you to Aaron Kent and Charlie Baylis for giving Shapeshifter the finest of homes.

LAY, OUT YOUR UNREST